A Village

Hoveringham, Caythor
Thurgarton and ̶ ̶ ̶ ̶ ̶ y

on old picture postcards

David Ottewell

Hoveringham

1. The man pushing his bicycle is leaving Hoveringham by Gonalston Lane. The house he has just passed is Bentwell House, which was built in 1900 so was very new when this photograph was taken. Card published by J.H. Scott of Bulcote.

£3.50

Introduction

This volume in the "Yesterday's Nottinghamshire" series focuses on a cluster of villages situated between Nottingham and Southwell, adjacent to the western bank of the River Trent running upstream from Hazelford to Gunthorpe. Many of the early settlers in this area would have arrived by river and put down roots so that they could exploit the Trent for food, transport and power. A number of watermills were later sited on the Trent and its tributaries like the Dover Beck. Settlements that grew up close to the river went on to serve its needs as it became a major commercial highway, and latterly a source of sport and recreation. Even today, the five villages featured attract many visitors, initially drawn by the lure of the nearby river.

The postcards used as illustrations for this book are an ideal resource, covering as they do events and developments in the villages over the past century. The 'Golden Age' of picture postcards was from 1902-14, and many of the best images were published in this period. Though they declined in use and popularity after 1918, cards continued to be published throughout the 20th century, reflecting everyday life. Examples in this volume come from national publishers such as Raphael Tuck or Blum & Degen, regional firms like the Doncaster Rotophoto Co. or C. & A.G. Lewis of Nottingham, and the prolific local postcard publisher J. Henry Scott of Bulcote, who toured the area photographing locations and events.

I hope the postcards featured here prompt many memories of times past.

David Ottewell
December 2000

Front cover: J. Henry Scott of Bulcote was on hand to record with his camera the momentous occasion when Hoveringham's new clock was installed on the Post Office wall on 28th October 1913. The building doubled as J.T. Berry's grocer shop. Most of the village's children, along with a number of adults, have been invited to pose for the photo. The card was written by Elsie at Laburnum Cottage, Hoveringham, and posted to Bleasby later that year.

Back cover (top): Sand's Photo Series published this postcard of Beck Street, Thurgarton in the 1920's. It gives a close up view of one of the many bridges which gave access from Beck Street across the beck to the adjacent houses. A number of children have come out to watch the photographer at work.

(bottom): a card of Bleasby's football team (helpfully captioned) in the 1905-06 season, published by Howard Barrett of Southwell. It was posted at Nottingham in February 1906.

Designed and published by
Reflections of a Bygone Age,
Keyworth, Nottingham 2000

**Printed by Adlard Print
& Reprographics Ltd**

HOVERINGHAM CHURCH, NOTTS.

2. An Edwardian view of St. Michael's Church, Hoveringham, which was designed by William Knight of Nottingham and opened in 1865, replacing an earlier church that had been demolished. The feature single bellcote can clearly be seen.

3. A view of St. Michael's Church from the opposite direction, with Gonalston Lane disappearing into the distance. Above the main door is a stone carving depicting St. Michael defending the church from evil. The postcard was published in Sand's Photo Series about 1920.

4. In the 17th century a house was built by the side of the Trent at Hoveringham for the ferrymen. It is understandable that many of the travellers sought refreshment, so by 1832 an inn had been established on the site. The boathouse (white building) was demolished in the 1960's. This card was postally used at Hoveringham in December 1907.

5. A closer view to the previous card. Written in 1925, the message runs *"You will recognise this spot Charlie. We have taken a few walks along the river side. We are getting nice weather. Spent a day at Newark and another at Nottingham last week. The bus passes the gate every day to various places"*. The building on the right was a boathouse in the first part of the 20th century, but it was originally a mortuary where bodies were stored prior to being taken to Nottingham for burial. Card published by Doncaster Rotophoto Co. Ltd.

6.The original pub here was called the "Old Ferry House", later changed to "The Old Elm Tree". It attracted large crowds and had a ballroom for 150 guests. It was closed in 1988 and is now divided into apartments. The gentleman and his dog on this postcard appear to be enjoying the view of the Trent. In the past it was the tradition that the local farmers paid their rents to their landlords, Trinity College Cambridge, at the "Elm Tree."

7. A pre-World War One card by J.H. Scott of Bulcote showing "The Marquis of Granby" Inn which took its name from one of the sons of the Duke of Rutland, who was based at Belvoir Castle.

8. This Doncaster Rotophoto Co. postcard, posted in 1926, is looking the opposite way to the previous card and features the three buildings past the "Marquis of Granby". The nearest is called "The Nook". The shop is now a private residence, known as "Lilac Cottage", whilst the farthest building is appropriately known as "The White House" *(see illus. 14 for a 1906 view of these properties).*

9. Further down Hoveringham Main Street, and on the opposite side to the previous buildings, is the village Post Office, constructed by a local builder in 1888. This postcard shows it c. 1907, with what was probably the grocer's delivery horse and cart outside. Sand's Photo Series postcard.

HOVERINGHAM VILLAGE.

10. An interesting comment by the writer of this postcard of the Post Office, sent to Southly Street in Nottingham on August 22nd 1906, runs *"I am coming down by the twenty past six train tonight"*. What an efficient postal service!

POST OFFICE, HOVERINGHAM, NOTTS.

11. A card of the Post Office after the installation of the clock (see front cover). Published in Sand's Photo Series, it was posted to Mablethorpe in August 1924.

12. The crossroads at Hoveringham on a Scott postcard posted to Ireland in August 1914, just after the outbreak of the First World War. The young lady writing it made no mention of this, however.

13. The girl is standing outside a building near the Post Office. The postcard's writer says on September 7th 1909: *"I send you this postcard just to let you see what part of the village I am staying at, you will notice the gate against the girl in white that is the entrance to the house of which I am staying"* (sic).

14. E. Parr's bakers and confectioners shop in 1906, with his horse-drawn delivery vehicle outside. Dawson's shop is next door; both are now private houses *(compare this card with illus. 8).*

15. A Doncaster Rotophoto Co. postcard looking back up Main Street. The house to the left remains today, although it is now painted white and faces a row of newer housing.

16. For many years the impressive thatched cottage featured on this card from the Doncaster Rotophoto Company Ltd served refreshments to people drawn to the village by its proximity to the River Trent. This card was sent from nearby Gonalston in 1937.

17. Station Road leads from Hoveringham to Thurgarton station, which serves the two villages. The man in the picture is standing on Station Road. Harry, writing the card to Jennie on September 10th 1909, says *"Just to let you know that there is two trains leaves here for Notts, one at a quarter to eleven and one at two o'clock"* (sic).

18. A meet of the local hunt gathered outside Hoveringham Hall on January 26th 1927. The original building dates from the late 17th century with numerous additions over the years. It has been in the Nell family for many years.

19. Powered by water, the mill at Hoveringham had a large water wheel built by the Newark firm of Wakes and Lamb. After the Second World War, electricity took over as the source of power. The card is no 362 in the 'Clumber' series dating from about 1907.

20. Kneeton Hill at Hoveringham on a postcard published by London firm Blum & Degen about 1907.

21. The lads of Hoveringham football team in 1925-26. No doubt some readers will recognise relatives on this postcard.

Caythorpe

22. These children are standing on the bridge which carried the road from Lowdham to Hoveringham over the Dover Beck and into the village of Caythorpe. The postcard by J.H. Scott of Bulcote was posted from Nottingham to Loughborough on 25th May 1916.

23. Rising near Blidworth, the Dover Beck makes its way to the River Trent which it joins near Caythorpe. This card by C & A.G. Lewis of Nottingham captures people paddling, fishing and boating.

24. A much changed view of the Main Street through Caythorpe looking towards "The Black Horse." The cottage to the left has been demolished. Beyond it the cart is just passing Marton cottage. To the right the building that resmbles a shed has now gone, and the dwelling past it, the old mill, is much altered. 'Clumber' series no. 476.

25. It is claimed that the highwayman, Dick Turpin, hid in the "Black Horse", which was originally three cottages. The Branston family bought the pub in 1868 and sold it to the local company Shipstones in the 1880's. From then until the 1950's the family acted as tenants. On this advertising card, Mrs F. Branston is listed as proprietress. By the late 1950's the "Black Horse" had been tidied up and the brewery had a much more discreet advertising sign. At this time the Branston family left and Jack Sherwin, grandson of the famous Nottinghamshire wicketkeeper, Mordecai Sherwin, became licencee.

26. A water mill has stood on the Dover Beck at Caythorpe since medieval times. The one pictured on this 1924 card by C. & A. G. Lewis of Nottingham dates from the middle of the 18th century. From the First World War until it was closed in 1952, the mill was operated by George Gregory and known locally as Gregory's Mill.

Gunthorpe

New Lock, Gunthorpe. No. 2958.

27. From the 1820's Gunthorpe had been a setting down point for goods transported up and down the Trent. In 1925 Nottingham Corporation built the new lock at Gunthorpe which was manually operated. Card by C. & A. G. Lewis.

Gunthorpe Bridge.

28. On May 16th 1873 Earl Manvers laid the foundation stone for Gunthorpe Toll bridge. Its ends were built of stone, some of which came from the Old Trent Bridge in Nottingham, whilst the middle was constructed of iron. The total cost, including the toll house on the Gunthorpe side, was £8,229 13s 6d. This postcard features a view by Spree of the Toll Bridge from the East Bridgford side. It was opened by the chairman of the Gunthorpe Bridge Company, Mr W.H. Martin J.P. on 18th June 1875. Initially the tolls were 11d horse and vehicle, 3d horse, 1d foot.

Opening New Bridge. Gunthorpe. Notts.

29. In 1924 work began on a new bridge over the Trent at Gunthorpe. It was sited about a quarter of a mile up river from the old bridge. The opening of the bridge was a big occasion locally, producing a large crowd to see the Prince of Wales perform the ceremony on 17th November 1927. The Nottingham photographer Spree captured the event for posterity, and postcards were quickly on sale to satisfy local demand. This one was sent from East Bridgford in November 1927.

Approach to Green, Gunthorpe

Copyright GNPE. II.

30. Turning at the edge of Gunthorpe bridge, the road brings you down parallel to the river to the "Unicorn Hotel" and the Green, which is the land to the right. In the far distance can be seen the old toll house. Card published by Raphael Tuck of London.

31. An advertising card for the "Unicorn Hotel" dating from prior to 1927 as the old toll bridge is one of the selected views. The proprietor, W.H. Edwards, had the cards printed for publicity purposes. It is interesting that C.B. Wells has taken over as proprietor and has put his own name on the card.

32. River Trent, Gunthorpe, on a postcard published by A.W. Bourne of Leicester. Since the photo was taken in the late 1950's there have been a number of changes. The row of three cottages joined to the "Unicorn" have been incorporated into the pub with a white frontage and similar pointed upper windows. The building at the end next to the cottages has been demolished.

NEAR THE
"HOTEL UNICORN"
GUNTHORPE.

33. Near the "Unicorn Hotel" - an early advertising postcard, possibly a little idyllic compared with the reality, to extol the virtures of the walks around the hotel. It was sent to someone at the "Beauchief Hotel" near Sheffield in September 1903.

The Green, Gunthorpe.

34. A card from Raphael Tuck and Sons Ltd. The Green is a small stretch of grass running between the river and the river road. The sign advertises "Riverside Tea Gardens". Today a modern bungalow occupies the site of the former Tea Gardens.

GUNTHORPE, NOTTS.   LIGHTHOUSE CAFÉ, AND GREEN

35. This building began life in 1875 as the tollhouse for the original toll bridge. Obviously it became redundant when the bridge was closed in the 1920's. It became a refreshment house, initially called, as here, "Lighthouse Cafe" and later "Mr Toad's".

36. A.W. Bourne of Leicester captured this early 1960's view of the Post Office Stores. The message written on the back of the card is interesting: *"You can see where we've got to: Guess What? I've brought an old piano! Its going in my bedroom, its a bit scratched but musically perfect".*

Lowdham Road, Gunthorpe.

37. The road taking traffic from the A46 Fosse Way to Lowdham over the new Gunthorpe Bridge has been very busy since its opening in the 1920's. It is not suprising, therefore, that a garage was soon established by this road to cater for the needs of passing motorists.

38. "The Hall", Gunthorpe. On entering the village, this imposing building appears on your left. It appears older than it actually is: parts date from the 18th century, but most of what can be seen, including the castellated tower, was added a hundred years later. Card no. 86 in the 'Clumber' series. The unusual shape of Gunthorpe Hall naturally attracted the attention of visitors to the village, and it was much photographed.

39. St John the Baptist Church was designed by the well-known Nottingham architect T.C. Hine. It was built in 1850 at a cost of £500. This postcard, published by Raphael Tuck, was sent from the village in July 1948.

40. A card in the extensive Raphael Tuck series of the village dating from just after the Second World War. Unfortunately, most of the views, like this one of the park, lack animation.

41. A superb postcard of the horse and cart belonging to Thomas Bros. at Gunthorpe Dairy, which claimed to supply *"New Milk Direct from the Farm"*. Anonymously published pre-1918 card of the transport in an unidentified nearby town.

Thurgarton

42. The memorial to local Thurgarton people who gave their lives in the First World War was built by the side of the main road facing the "Coach and Horses" public house. The building behind the war memorial is today the site of the village post office and shop.

43. The horse and cart are travelling unconcernedly down the centre of the Southwell Road in Thurgarton. Above the cart can be seen the sign of the second pub in the village, "The Red Lion". The card is in 'Sand's Photo Series' and was posted in December 1917.

44. This anonymously-produced card sent to Derby in 1910 shows the boy about to walk the cow past The Lodge and through the gates into the park.

CHURCH & PRIORY. THURGARTON 17-6

45. An Augustinian priory was founded at Thurgarton between 1119 and 1139 by Ralph Deyncourt, a wealthy landowner. At the Dissolution of the Monasteries in 1538 it passed into the hands of William Cooper, who demolished some of the priory and built himself a family home. Card by Doncaster Rotophoto Co.

46. The Water Garden at Thurgarton Priory. An anonymously-produced card sent from Thurgarton on 1st July 1914 showing some of the attractive features in the parkland around the Priory.

47. Picturesque Beck Street in Thurgarton. It obviously takes its name from the beck which runs parallel to the road. It leads from Thurgarton to nearby Hoveringham. The postcard sent from Newark has an appropriate message considering its posting date of 31st August 1939: *"Hope you are having a good time in spite of troubled times"*.

48. The Convalescent Home, Thurgarton, the last building at the Southwell end of the village. Posted on 7th June 1919, this postcard shows the house which for many years was used to look after children recovering from tuberculosis. It was specially designed to be child-friendly, with all the light switches at a low level. It is now a private house.

49. An Edwardian postcard showing a train on the Lincoln branch of the Midland Railway coming into Thurgarton station. At this time Job Frederick Fisher is recorded as being the station master.

Bleasby

50. A postcard showing the road from Thurgarton as it enters Goverton. The pony and trap is drawn up by the wall bordering Goverton House. The card was postally used at Newark in May 1908.

51. In Edwardian times, Goverton was a small hamlet. Here J.H. Scott of Bulcote has photographed the main thoroughfare. Goverton Cottage is seen to the left, with the eaves of the White House, situated beyond, just visible over the roof top. The postcard was sent from Newark to Algiers on 1st November 1909.

52. The area of Bleasby known as Notown. The large house with the Tudor decoration almost completely hides the chapel behind it, which dates from 1879. The postcard was sent from Katie to her mother, Mrs Lidgett, at Gibsmere in October 1910 from Holbeach, telling of the train journey there.

53. A winter scene showing the first house on Gypsy Lane, Bleasby, with its distinctive window bays and mock Tudor decoration. The building protruding between this house and the "Waggon and Horses" beyond is an old wheelwright's shop.

54. The "Waggon and Horses" public house at Bleasby, built in the late 18th century.

easby.

55. Bleasby Church, looking from the Northern aspect of St Mary's Church on this card by J.H. Scott written in 1907. Although the church dates from the 13th century, it has been extensively restored, including on three occasions in Victorian times. As in many parts of the country, Bleasby is now part of a team ministry.

56. An Edwardian view of the railway station at Bleasby in winter time with a train drawing into the station. The line between Nottingham and Lincoln, on which Bleasby stands, was opened by the Midland Railway Company in 1846. Card published by J.H. Scott c.1907.

Bleasby, Notts.

57. Mrs Lidgett at Glebe Farm, Gibsmere, was sent this postcard on 17th April 1912. With telephones still not widely available, the sending of a postcard was the most effective and cheapest method of communicating with people. St Mary's tower can be seen peeping between the trees.

Gibsmere Bleasby

58. Gibsmere is a small hamlet near Bleasby. This fine postcard, published by J.H. Scott, probably features most of the population in 1908.

59. The hounds at Bleasby Hall. When this card was posted in December 1908, Captain Marmaduke Langdale Kelham R.N.J.P. resided at the Hall and was Lord of the Manor. Meetings of the Hunt were a regular feature of life in the area. The 1908 Kelly's Directory for Nottinghamshire describes the Hall thus: *"a large building of brick faced with cement with a central facade flanked by two embattled towers built about the 17th century and surrounded by attractive pleasure gardens"*.

60. Bleasby Village. The view in Edwardian times with the horse, cart and men pausing outside the "Fisherman's Rest" public house. The building in the foreground is Court Cottage. 'Clumber' series postcard no. 275.